AN IRON RING
PUBLICATION

WEALTH

A practical manual combining
the understanding of
what it is, how to attain it, how to
keep it flowing combining
deconstruction of previous
doctrine and reconstruction
through PULSE WORK and
Directional Sorcery
By

SORCERESS CAGLIASTRO

AN IRON RING PUBLICATION

WEALTH

.... what it is, how to attain it, how to keep it flowing....

Transcript from the

WEALTH SEDATION

class on 9/6/16

copyright 2016

AUTHORS FORWARD

This book is built from a transcript of a class called WEALTH SEDATION. Sedations are single classes offered to individuals of all levels of study (including people completely new to the work). In the Sedation, participants experience two types of opportunity. The first half or so of the class introduces the materials and all the definitions, examples etc. that one requires to understand the broader gaze of the work at hand. Then the instruction leans more toward participation as the structure of the Sedation is revealed. Secondly, students participate in a timed process where they are experiencing the work first hand by following the process. It is called a Sedation not because anyone is actually Sedated, but rather because the timed exercise allows the student to participate in the process and gather their own customized data.

Readers of the transcript will have the same opportunities by reading carefully through the material and doing the exercises just as they are listed. Herein you will find the full transcript, including the description of the Sedation, and the actual Sedation with timed directives. Also note, that by the end of 2016, the recordings for all of the Sedations will also be available.

That being said, this is a transcript, not a novel. It is only lightly edited so that readers will get the full volume of material with the best possible attention to clarity and detail. The typeface in all of my books is large, as my students may enjoy working at their altars (no deity or divinity implied – for students of the Science of Sorcery, altars are simply places set aside for the work), their candlelight, and their general sense of knowing the value of night. The structure also allows for room to write by spacing the work with enough blank space for notes.

This book may also be thought of as a workbook – write in it, utilize it for your full exploration of this work.

Remember that all of my books come from the place of understanding your Blood, your life force, your Sacred Elixir. Therefore you should NOT SHARE this book, and from that point of view I suggest that you consider anointing this, and any of my books with a simple dot of your Blood to hone it to you and to make it your own.

Use this circle to anoint this book, and take ownership of the knowledge herein...

This book is dedicated to N who pointed out luxury and made it so terribly important......

SORCERESS CAGLIASTRO
Blood Sorceress, Success,
Necromancer in the hands of 9

WEALTH

The subject of WEALTH, what it is, how to attain it, how to keep it flowing.... all of these questions are often the subjects of consistent inquiries...

In this SEDATION we will look at those issues, and focus the teaching on SOLUTION METHODS specifically. These methods are based on a set of STRUCTURES and associated Pillar/Sorcery techniques. Although this work is quite useful to individuals who practice the Science of Sorcery, this particular Sedation utilizes pulse markers and Directional Sorcery, which is a basic understanding of the Polarities. People taking this class DO NOT HAVE TO own other books, nor do they have to have a proficiency in Directional Sorcery as the basics are implied in this transcript. However if one chooses to advance their knowledge about the powerful Pillar of Directional Sorcery, There is an extensive covering of Directional Sorcery in two of the books –

The Science of Sorcery Beginner Course: Vol I, Blood Sorcery and Directional Sorcery Class Transcripts

As well as more advanced manual

16 Rooms And the use of BLACKHOUSES: Advanced DIRECTIONAL SORCERY

Regarding the content of **this** Sedation about WEALTH, much of this has not been previously taught in this manner, so this is a single teaching opportunity which is built to cure the issues which stand in the way of attaining wealth by doing the work herein and allowing it to deconstruct and then reconstruct your "presence" within WEALTH. This is a completely different approach to the attainment of wealth then anything you have previously explored. Through guidance you will be brought through the experience of BEING in the sensations of WEALTH which may have previously felt as if those opportunities belonged to other.... Attendees will be guided through COLLECTIVE CONSCIOUSNESS into the focus to make these re-established and powerful connections.

This class is useful for Beginners and Advanced Students as it is my desire to have a substantial group from which to utilize the font of COLLECTIVE CONSCIOUSNESS.

Tonight I will bring the attendees through a sensation based experienced where we will focus **outside** of our accepted territory and physical selves to find an alignment with the WEALTH. I will first define the **STRUCTURES** that allow us to operate in a framework of WEALTH- then I will work through a timed removal of non-structural items, and an insertion of abilities that will clear the way for the acceptance of WEALTH.

AFTER TONIGHT you will think of wealth in a very different way than you have before. Combine that with functional Sorcery practices **and WEALTH becomes just another part of you –** as **opposed** to that which is always just out of reach or difficult to attain.

Let's begin....

Have a notebook available....

The first question that must be asked is are you living in an **ACCEPTABLE LOSS?** By this I mean is the energy you have around WEALTH based on an acceptance that wealth is cyclical, attached to luck, based on being given it from other sources (as opposed to your own power) or waiting for the sources willingness to pay out? For you does WEALTH have something to do with how hard you have worked – or even worse – you have some thought that your wealth is based in some emotional equation about "deserving"?

(Utilize the templates in the **ANNEX** of this book for access to all the materials discussed going forward. COPY the page of blank sigil circles or draw your own.)

Cut out a blank sigil circle and put the words **ACCEPTABLE LOSS** in the center of that sigil circle and we will use it later even if you don't think that description sound like you.

SCAPEGOAT PROCESS

What is your definition of wealth? Ask yourself and write the shortest definition you can think of... Tonight will help you to see if you are you in the scapegoat process?

Acceptance that wealth is only inherited, comes to people with amazing educations, comes to people from certain socio-economic strata, is derived from WHO you know, has an association with one's physical attractiveness or is an outcome of the draw of right place and right time will keep you from WEALTH. Or, if you have some thought that your access to WEALTH is based in some class strata equation about "deserving" then there is much to deconstruct. Write the words SCAPEGOAT in a circle and we will use it later even if you don't think that description sound like you.

WEALTH or the lack thereof, comes from knowing and manipulating through Sorcery these structures:

THE STRUCTURES:

SOURCE "BELIEF"

JEALOUSY/ENVY TRAP

ANCHOR ITEMS

RECIPIENT TERRITORY

IRREVERENCE (ego, thoughts of worthiness, an idea about life behavior

SEEDING and associated Pillar techniques. (we will use Blood Sorcery and Directional Sorcery)

I will go through those definitions, then expand the definition of the Anchor Item and associated materials.

Then we will look at that in visual contrast to SOURCE "BELIEF"

Then we will look at RECIPIENT TERRITORY

Then we will look at SEEDING and EXPLAIN the preference for specific pillar techniques

The we will begin to look at IRREVERENCE

THEN we will work all of these STRUCTURES in a way through utilizing Pulse Checking and the polarities which will show you how fast the work expands your qualification to control your own wealth.

First let's define WEALTH. WEALTH is, first of all, **good**. To have wealth one must have selfishness, so let's start there for a moment.

> **Selfishness is quite simply the direction of energy and therefore the direction of Sorcery onto the self.**

It is just that simple. I often refer to the well-known directive that one gets in air travel. I will refer to it here. So when one is on an airplane, and there is a situation that causes the oxygen masks to drop – one puts the mask on the SELF FIRST so that they can then take care of any dependent persons such as children, with whom they are travelling. This is vital as one cannot take care of others if one passes out.

This is not a self-help lesson. I say that first because it is important for you to know that this is, a loose two phase process, a deconstruction based in your reaction to NOT HAVING, which is a deconstruction of SOURCE BELIEF - followed by an insertion of ANCHOR ITEMS, RECIPIENT

TERRITORY, IRREVERNECE and SEEDING, and all associated facets

Tonight as I always do in Sedations - I will be doing Sorcery to assist you into the polarities, as we will be utilizing directional sorcery as we get into the work. Readers of this work will find that mechanism is built into the language of the text, so if you are struggling, read the portion aloud...

Let's get to the definitions...

SOURCE "BELIEF"

Now those of you who know my work know that I do not use the word "Belief" unless I am discussing something that I consider to be bogus and without merit.

> Belief is something that is attached to that which does not provide enough data to be proven.

People believe in gods, people believe in Karma, people believe in the goodness or evil of others, people believe that certain groups or types of people always act in a certain way, and people tend to believe that WEALTH is defined only by money, and that WEALTH is attained only by some self-established OR doctrine related baseline of deserving. If you accept these "beliefs" then WEALTH is NOT in your hands.

DOCTRINE

Many associate WEALTH with greed. Is having WEALTH greedy? Is it taboo? Does it belong to others and if so are they the bad guys? Is it somehow tied to a lack of humility?

> **No, wealth is just wealth – and if you have it you can live more freely...**

JEALOUSY/ENVY TRAP

> Jealousy is just a deflection to a question about deserving filtered through judgements about others.

I have a **very disharmonious** association with jealousy and envy. Very Disharmonious... I do not have jealousy or envy with anyone – all that shows up for me if someone has something I desire is this: how do I utilize what I HAVE to gain that? I have **zero connection** to or concern with the person who already has that which I desire in my approach – my connection is **only** to the attainment, not even to the item itself.

With that frame of focus, the energy that I use goes entirely to the thing - **requiring** – and nothing is wasted on the individual who already has that thing – as what's to be gained by focusing in that direction?

> To involve the self in jealousy or envy is to guarantee that there will be– going forward – an increase in distance between the self and wealth.

Of whom are you Jealous? – turn the answer to this into a **SEEDING** which means write down in an open sigil circle (see ANNEX) the name or names of people or situations about which you have a sensation of jealousy. Be HONEST with yourself – you are alone and no one is watching your choices....)

ANCHOR ITEMS

They are called ANCHOR ITEMS as they will anchor us to the experience of having through mimicry and triggers. There are two kinds of Anchor Items. One is something you already have and have obtained against what you would perceive as "all odds" and one that you have kept in the fantasy lane. Everyone has both of those. Allow me to expand on this...

Obtained Anchor Items are those that you already have, which you have obtained by some transaction that felt as if it had superior value, and of which you feel you obtained within a framework that has not been simple to replicate. Think broadly, this framework can be financial, career based, erotic, romantic, or a Sorcery based achievement. Example - If you are a real estate agent then it is that one great hit you had where the price was too high, yet the right buyer came in and **wham** you nailed it. If you are a collector it is the ring or object you obtained at just the right price or won in an auction – or the lover you thought was out of range for you - or in a bidding situation where you felt you had superpowers – or the most **deadly** of assumptions – that you were in the right place at the right time. It doesn't matter which of those it is however everyone has something or some experience that they hold as the fish that

didn't get away.... Place that thing or things in a sigil circle. Set it aside.

Secondly the FANTASY ANCHOR ITEM. To be clear = this is not a "wish list" – this is not the thing that you feel you cannot ever have however you fanaticize about it – because those are either NOT things you have an expectation of receiving – OR they are the things that you have set so far off that they are not really within your Recipient Territory (which we will discuss next).... The FANTASY ANCHOR ITEM is the thing you feel is just past your fingertips, because you can feel and see your fingertips, and you can see the space between them and that which you desire - so it is already a realistic construct... This is the thing you desire and see yourself attaining – you just don't have the **mechanism** for **HOW** that will be accomplished. Note that as you move forward in the work of WEALTH, and as these Fantasy Anchor Items are attained, you will require new ones, however the mimicry of the attainment of the one we set into motion **tonight** is the trigger force – so when we get there remember to enact that trigger....Name it and make sure the trigger is usable....

Place your Fantasy Anchor Item in one sigil circle, and the **TRIGGER** word that best describes it in another circle. In this Sedation and going forward you will be using that trigger for the attainment of all replacement fantasy anchor items ...

RECIPIENT TERRITORY

This is the "where you are" of the WEALTH process – your power of place in WEALTH. We are trained that WEALTH is somehow tied to a lack of humility and all of the doctrine we have been subject to. And if it is – in your individual minds tied to a lack of humility then one of two solutions is required. First – we require to either redefine humility if that is something that you desire to be part of the description of the self. Example – if I have 7 million dollars, do I lose humility? Can I no longer be humble? That question is a loaded one because there are 2 solutions. Secondly, if humility is important to you – than preset whatever that word means to you be able to be something that occurs **within wealth NOT only in poverty**. The other side of the answer is that HUMILITY may NOT be a requirement for you. This sedation will help you to see that and own it - Either way – within your RECIPIENT TERRITORY – DECIDE, as you will see if you genuinely require these kinds of facets (humility, humbleness, grace, gratitude) and if you do – place markers for them. Place them on sigil circles either way as we will use them in the Sedation.

My advice at the Sorcery level is that this is disingenuous. When we discover WEALTH – how to obtain it and how to maintain it – what happens is similar to what happens in Death – we become more of who we are.

> **THE GREATEST BARRICADE TO WEALTH IS THE ASSUMPTION THAT IT WILL MAKE YOU INTO SOMETHING YOU ARE NOT.**
>
> **THIS** is the real baseline for a fear of success...

The fact is that it will **not** make you into anything – it will only take away barricades between you and "permission". By this I mean you will show up in your authentic self – and that self may be driven more by possessions and enjoyment, by beauty and self-satisfaction, by providing excess for yourself and for your family, by opulence, by having time to think, by allowing for the down time that working 24 hours a day does not allow – and thusly you will be able to learn about who you are.... The effort here is to broaden your RECIPIENT TERRITORY to a location known as EVERYWHERE.

Place words like humility and humbleness or words of that nature in a circle/s.

IRREVERENCE

This category is one of those where I tell you how it works and everything you know of tells you that what I am saying is not how it works....

I tell you that there is a broad difference between mimicry, mentors and models of behavior and you tell me that although that sounds great – it makes no sense. What comes into play here is ego, thoughts of worthiness, an idea about life behavior.

When we mimic, have mentors, or contradict models of behavior we are acting in irreverence toward the distinct doctrine we are handed. We are simply told not to do that. That instruction is external control and keeps us away from WEALTH.

Evidence - if it bothers you that a skateboarder or someone who plays poker has a great and conscious understanding of - and experience with WEALTH – then you have been TRICKED BY THE STORY of how wealth is experienced – not attained – experienced, and that is why you have judgement or jealously about people who have WEALTH who do not fit your definition of people who deserve it as they do not APPEAR to have worked hard enough or played by the rules...

Be honest with yourself about this – as it will serve you to remove this judgement...

So write the words TRICKED BY THE STORY (how you were told WEALTH is attained) inside of a circle and we will use it in the timed portion of the sedation.

SEEDING

Has the exhaustion of loss allowed for you to have a location in your **RECIPIENT TERRITORY** that makes it ok for you to lose what you have had – or to see what you have as generally losable? Let's look at something that can be really **inappropriate** to look at if you are subject to political correctness. Let's revisit ENVY. If you find that you are envious of "idots" then you are missing a huge opportunity to utilize mimicry or 5th pillar work (for those who know the battery work).

Right there is the data – and if we look at the data through our own filter then the data is exact, customized for us to see our own blocks. Think about this... How does that guy who just joined the firm make such great sales? How is a rapper paid millions of dollars to talk into the mic? How does someone fall into huge amounts of money and not do anything with it? How do I jump in front of the DNA train and get past what was told to me about WEALTH? All of this is handled by SEEDING your personal RECIPIENT TERRITORY with mimicry addresses and one of which has to be a location that represents HAVING and not just KNOWING. IT MUST BECOME TANGIBLE....

Mimicry - in that location exists someone who has great WEALTH – tailored of course to the TYPE of WEALTH you would like to have. By this I mean look at specifics. Do you desire the type of wealth that comes with fame, responsibility, fast pay outs? Do you desire the kind of wealth that you have to build on to sustain or the kind that delivers big numbers fast and then the future is up to you? Or do you desire the kind of wealth that lends itself toward a less public life?

Seeding involves placing into your Recipient Territory mimic addresses – and in these mimic addresses we place those examples/situation/people (and I really suggest you use people) who represent the exact type of attainment you desire. Their

industry does not have to be your industry –
their **accomplishment level** is the mimicry you
require. Once you install them – then, after
you do this work all the through, you will
either continue in your industry and make
enormous strides OR you will find yourself
changing industries as THAT will lead you to
the WEALTH that is now available....

I myself have been very successful in an
industry that is first and foremost male,
secondly filled with regurgitated codexes and
nonsense – "sudden shamans", and thirdly –
tend to be white light, glitter and very divinity
and deity based OR everyone is trying to be
dark superheroes.... Now you all know I rarely
if ever bring gender into anything- however in
the scheme of things, if one took boundaries
as norms, (YIKES) or even as hurdles – then
I would never have made my work public
because in the accepted structure - My work
should only have been accepted if offered by
a man, preferably a scientist with 20 degrees,
who is over 50, straight, has a few kids and who

panders to church on the weekend. However, as you know, it was not...as I am the polar opposite.... The point is that I looked at all of those authors and decided that I would **NOT SEED** my Recipient Territory with any of that – I would rather look to industries where women who saw something from a point of view that was traditionally not accepted as theirs to see – and I realized **THAT** energy would best seed my Recipient Territory.... Some of you know who at least one of those seed individuals is....and she is most certainly **NOT** from my industry....

So set the names of individuals whose **SUCCESS** you desire to mimic into several circles and set them aside....

PILLAR TECHNIQUES

Let's discuss the pillar techniques. For this work there are many options going forward....

I suggest you utilize your Blood. You are altering your DNA of WEALTH and I say that not on the esoteric, The Secret or 4 Agreements way... as I do not have a handle on the internal destruction caused by the open ended hoping and wishing.... I say that in the way that we alter our DNA by the change of the flow of Desire, Require, Thoughts, Ideas, Intentions and work though the Pillars as filters.

You will be utilizing a basic aspect of Blood Sorcery - your pulse. You will use it to "read" for changes – and I will run the timing so you will not have to concern yourself with anything but the counting. (Readers of this transcript will require a stopwatch which most phones offer.) Then we will use DIRECTIONAL SORCERY to simultaneously break away some of the bonds that hold individuals away from wealth – and build or increase the bonds to those that place us within these STRUCTURES of wealth... Those new to Directional Sorcery will be fine here – this

Sedation (and therefore this transcript) provide all that is necessary at this point....

THE STRUCTURE'S POLARITIES

I will read through these before we begin the timed COLLECTIVE CONSCIOUSNESS version during which I will be doing Sorcery for your permeability to these changes. Hearing these first will create a comfort zone as we move into the timed aspect of the Sedation. (Readers of this transcript will share in this experience through reading the SEDATION portion aloud before doing each of the 10 exercises.)

General Directional Sorcery Notes

SOUTH – remove

NORTH – attract

EAST – speed up

WEST – appropriate timing

Let's begin....read through these categories...and then we will do the work in the Timed portion of the same material...

SOURCE "BELIEF"

SOUTH - as it is our job to un-remember – the sensations of the following:

Lack, poverty, unworthiness, the engineering of guilt attached to WEALTH, a sensation that anyone else has control over our experience of having. For that we work South – and **create** broken bonds to those elements. Creating broken bonds is richer in outcome then breaking bonds. It is a doubled and therefore more powerful effort with a greater outcome.

Then – once that is done we will put **EVISCERATION OF MEMORIES** into the **NORTH**. This is a vital nuance. Often students come to me with all the right pieces and NOT all of the right Polarities. So, for example, if we put the sigil for **EVISCERATION OF MEMORIES** in the **SOUTH** - all we would accomplish is the breaking of bonds with the **ABILITY** to eviscerate these memories.

JEALOUSY/ENVY TRAP

We will work entirely **SOUTH** here – then **EAST**, then **SOUTH EAST** – This is "Remove it and remove it fast".

ANCHOR ITEMS

NORTH – for obvious reasons however I will expand on them – we are fulfilling a requirement that allows us to increase the bonds with not only the Anchor Items themselves – also with the IDEA aspect of Requirement. Desire is the uptake to Requirement just as Thoughts are the uptake to IDEAS, and IDEAS are the uptake to INTENTIONS.

RECIPIENT TERRITORY

The **RECIPIENT TERRITORY** is instinctual and will change...you will be drawing it on the compass plate – remember that this is **diagnostic** and shows what you have and have NOT included in your Recipient Territory. When doing so, it is important that you **observe** the polarities to which you are drawn.... This will assist you in the ability to know which of these structures are less enticing, thereby showing you which ones will require additional work.

IRREVERENCE

Ego, thoughts of worthiness, an idea about life behavior are at play here – **EAST** to jump start your RELATIONSHIP with Irreverence – then **NORTH** to increase your bonds – then ultimately **NORTH EAST**

SEEDING

First **NORTH** to establish the relationship between yourself and the process of SEEDING. Then **WEST** as appropriate timing is fully flexible. It is "languaged" as speeds up or slows down delivery. However, at this more advanced practice, you can take in this description – The West puts everything in a time release capsule, and as the body (the whole person) is ready the drug is released. NOTHING in all of the 5 pillars is more personalized – and I do mean nothing – than putting something for yourself in the WEST. The WEST is a full on relationship – a total commitment – not a one night stand. The WEST tells you – yes – I am in this for the duration. When you feel fully connected to the WEST, then we will bring the SEEDS NORTH WEST.

OK, take three minutes to cut out 2 pages of blanks. (Readers try to remain within the timeframes as well.) They have hexagons around them so that you can simply straight cut them quickly. They don't have to be perfect – they will be placed outside of the board – so don't worry about the size of them.

Also cut out the 4 additional sigils, 23 7 23 9 Forget and Eviscerate Doctrine. The compass board is left as is.

The three minutes start now.

SEDATION

We will be using pulse rate to note changes. Let me clarify "changes". This means that your pulse will either speed up or slow down OR your pulse power will feel stronger or weaker to the touch. When you take your pulse, note not only the count, but also the change in power. As placebo or suggestion has no part in my work, I will wait until the times session is over to tell you the relevance of faster, slower, weaker or stronger.

Use the COMPASS PLATE and place it in alignment with the actual polarities (North in the actual North).

TAKE YOUR PULSE – there will be a 10 second "readying" during which time you will feel your pulse – it is important to get in connection with that touch before the 60 second count so that it is comfortable and accurate, so the count will be 10 seconds – then I will say BEGIN COUNTING. Then you will Write down the count for the 60 seconds and after the first time you will also write weaker, stronger, same as the first time gives you your baseline. . OK – here is the 10 second readying – BEGIN ONE MINUTE

THE TIMING METHOD FOR ALL 9 SEDATIONS WILL BE THE SAME: I will read it now and then read it again after each instruction is read.

You will have 1 minute to place them. Do so consciously and know that I am using Sorcery for permeability so that the work is available to you. After that minute I will say 10 seconds – and in that 10 seconds set up your pulse.

Then I will say start and you will have 60 seconds to take your pulse. Then I will say stop and you will have 1 minute to write pulse results and thoughts.

1. Breathe – you will breathe for a full minute – it will feel like much more than a minute. ONE MINUTE

2. This is the first pulse, 10 seconds to get ready – ok BEGIN ONE MINUTE. Take 30 seconds to write # and strength impression.

3. **SOURCE "BELIEF"** – USE YOUR ACCEPTABLE LOSS SIGIL HERE. Place it in the SOUTH - as it is our job to un-remember the sensations of the following:
Lack, poverty, unworthiness, the engineering of guilt attached to wealth, a

sensation that anyone else has control over our experience of having. For that we work South – and create broken bonds to those elements.

You will have 1 minute to place them. Do so consciously and know that I am using Sorcery for permeability so that the work is available to you. After that minute I will say 10 seconds – and in that 10 seconds set up your pulse. Then I will say start and you will have 60 seconds to take your pulse. Then I will say stop and you will have 1 minute to write pulse results and thoughts.

4. PLACE the **SCAPEGOAT** and **EVISCERATION OF MEMORIES, S23 VII TO CHANGE OR UNEMPOWER GENETICS** and S23

IX ESCAPING OF DOCTRINE here as well into the **NORTH**. This is a vital nuance. Often students come to me with all the right pieces and NOT all of the right Polarities. So, for example, if we put the sigil for **EVISCERATION OF MEMORIES** in the **SOUTH** – all we would accomplish is the breaking of bonds with the **ABILITY** to eviscerate these memories.

You will have 1 minute to place them. Do so consciously and know that I am using Sorcery for permeability so that the work is available to you. After that minute I will say 10 seconds – and in that 10 seconds set up your pulse. Then I will say start and you will have 60 seconds to take your pulse. Then I will say stop and you will have 1 minute to write pulse results and thoughts.

5. **JEALOUSY/ENVY TRAP** **Place the Jealousy circles SOUTH** here – then bend **EAST**, then **SOUTH EAST** – This is "Remove it and remove it fast". You will have 1 minute to place them. Do so consciously and know that I am using Sorcery for permeability so that the work is available to you. After that minute I will say 10 seconds – and in that 10 seconds set up your pulse. Then I will say start and you will have 60 seconds to take your pulse. Then I will say stop and you will have 1 minute to write pulse results and thoughts.

6. **ANCHOR ITEMS – Place obtained anchor items and FANTASY ANCHOR ITEMS and the TRIGGER NORTH** – For obvious reasons however I will expand on them – we are fulfilling a requirement that allows us to increase the bonds with not only the Anchor Items themselves – also with the IDEA aspect of Requirement. Desire is the uptake to Requirement just as Thoughts are the uptake to IDEAS, and IDEAS are the uptake to INTENTIONS. You will have 1 minute to place them. Do so consciously and know that I am using Sorcery for permeability so that the work is available to you. After that minute I will say 10 seconds – and in that 10 seconds set up

your pulse. Then I will say start and you will have 60 seconds to take your pulse. Then I will say stop and you will have 1 minute to write pulse results and thoughts.

7. **RECIPIENT TERRITORY** The RECIPIENT TERRITORY is instinctual and will change...you will be drawing it on the compass plate – remember that this is diagnostic and shows what you have and have NOT included in your Recipient Territory. When doing so, it is important that you observe the polarities to which you are drawn.... This will assist you in the ability to know which of these structures are less enticing, thereby showing you which ones will require additional work. –

THINK LESS, FEEL MORE and draw your RECIPIENT TERRITORY. Pick up your words (humility etc.) and FEEL – do they or do they not have a place within your RECIPIENT TERRITORY? They may or may not. You will have 1 minute to place them. Do so consciously and know that I am using Sorcery for permeability so that the work is available to you. After that minute I will say 10 seconds – and in that 10 seconds set up your pulse. Then I will say start and you will have 60 seconds to take your pulse. Then I will say stop and you will have 1 minute to write pulse results and thoughts.

8. **IRREVERENCE** (ego, thoughts of worthiness, an idea about life behavior

Place your TRICKED BY THE STORY circle- **EAST** to jump start your RELATIONSHIP with Irreverence – then **NORTH** to increase your bonds – then ultimately **NORTH EAST** You will have 1 minute to place them. Do so consciously and know that I am using Sorcery for permeability so that the work is available to you. After that minute I will say 10 seconds – and in that 10 seconds set up your pulse. Then I will say start and you will have 60 seconds to take your pulse. Then I will say stop and you will have 1 minute to write pulse results and thoughts.

9. **SEEDING** Place your SEEDS in the **NORTH** to establish the relationship between yourself and the process of

SEEDING.   Then **WEST** as appropriate timing is fully flexible. It is "languaged" as speeds up or slows down delivery.   However, at this more advanced practice, you can take in this description – The West puts everything in a time release capsule, and as the body is ready the drug is released. NOTHING in all of the 5 pillars is more personalized – and I do mean nothing – than putting something for yourself in the WEST. The WEST also is a full on relationship – a total commitment – not a one-night stand. The WEST tells you – yes – I am in this for the duration. When you feel fully connected to the WEST, then we will bring the SEEDS NORTH WEST.   You will have 1 minute to place them. Do so consciously and know that I am using Sorcery for permeability so that the work is available to you. After that minute I will say 10 seconds – and in that 10 seconds set up your pulse. Then I will say start and you will have 60 seconds to take your pulse. Then I will say stop and you will have 1 minute to write pulse results and thoughts.

10.   Take your pulse again – 10 second warning – 60 sec pulse. Go. Write number and strength impression.. Now Breathe fir 60 seconds. Take your pulse again – 10 second warning – 60 sec pulse. Go. Write final number and strength impression..

DATA to help you to understand your pulse results....

FASTER AND MORE POWERFUL - fully engaged and attached to permeability – changes absorbed by the Blood

SLOWER AND WEAKER - struggling to learn and absorb

SLOWER AND MORE POWERFUL - Grasping the process and "downloading"

FASTER AND WEAKER - already in progress

ANNEX

23S IX **ESCAPING OF DOCTRINE**

from the book

"23 Sigils of Selfish Indulgence"

available on
amazon.com/author/sorceresscagliastro

23S VII CHANGE OR UN-EMPOWER
GENETICS

from the book

"23 Sigils of Selfish Indulgence"

available on
amazon.com/author/sorceresscagliastro

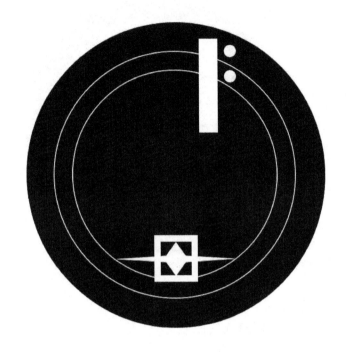

EVISCERATION OF MEMORIES

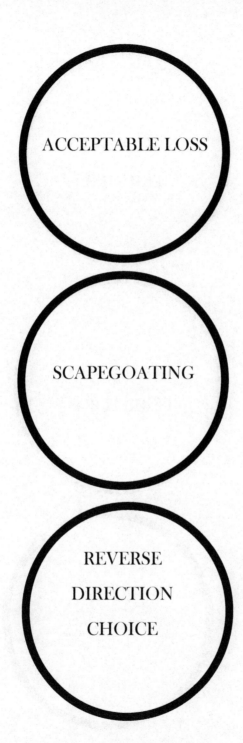

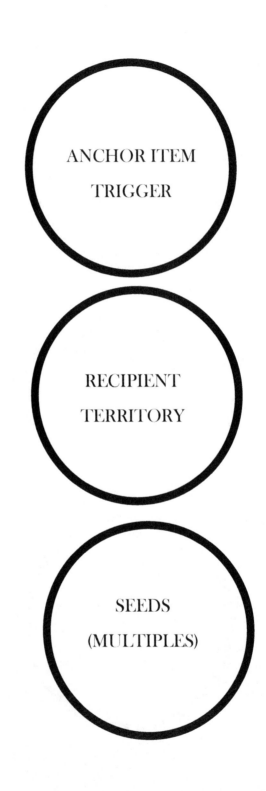

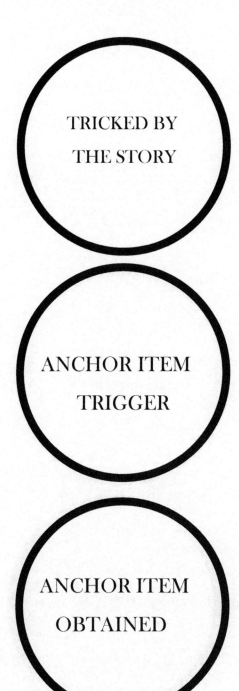

ANCHOR ITEM

FANTASY

USABLE TEMPLATE FOR HAND WRITTEN SIGIL CIRCLES

Copy MULTIPLE TIMES and cut out along hexagon lines for easy cutting

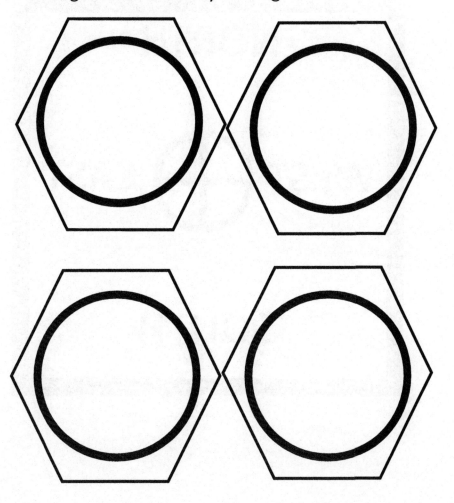

COMPASS PLATE

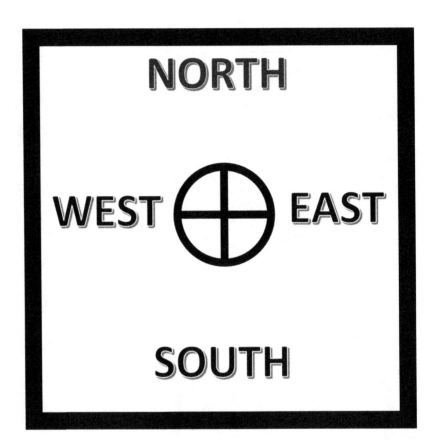

NOTES

NOTES

BIO AND BOOK CATALOG

SORCERESS CAGLIASTRO,
BLOOD SORCERESS, NECROMANCER IN THE
HANDS OF 9....

... author, publisher, lecturer, teacher, Daemon Handler, Necromancer, and Exorcist, creator of THE IRON RING, a Science of Sorcery practice through which to explore the broader gaze of the experience of Sorcery. It was created for and is taught to individuals of a mindset to learn Blood Sorcery, Necromancy, Divination, Directional Sorcery, The Static Practice, other Pillars and the broad gaze of the work. The Sorceress is a lifelong practitioner of and the foremost authority on Science of Sorcery, Blood Sorcery and the related Pillars of the Iron Ring Method…

The Sorceress has authored the Blood Sorcery Bibles Vol 1 and Vol 2 and many other books on the Science of Sorcery as well as fiction and screenplays based on her experiences with Daemons and the Disincarnate. Recently, through her publishing company North Sea Tales, the Sorceress has also published books under the project name of "Rescued Knowledge Project, A Cagliastro Endeavor". These are historical books of a broad gaze of interests. They are available in paperback and a few of them are currently available on the Kindle. All of her books are available on Amazon, keywords Sorceress Cagliastro or visit her amazon author page at amazon.com/author/sorceresscagliastro.

Classes with the Sorceress are available on live via live stream - however seating is limited, as her classes and teaching are very popular both in the United States and Internationally. Starting this year, she is offering "Learn As You Go", giving Beginner Students the chance to study and learn Blood Sorcery and the Science of Sorcery through the Pillars. That thorough six-month class offering, is taken on your time via recorded sessions, and students have the opportunity to meet individually on live feed (on line) with The Sorceress monthly as part of the program.

FOR FURTHER INFORMATION - OR FOR PRESS INQUIRIES

sorceresscagliastro@gmail.com

THE SORCERESS CAGLIASTRO,
Blood Sorceress, Necromancer in the hands of 9

For more information about The Science of Sorcery or to study with The Sorceress Cagliastro visit
www.cagliastrotheironring.com or

Email sorceresscagliastro@gmail.com

BOOKS BY
THE SORCERESS CAGLIASTRO

TITLES BY THE SORCERESS CAGLIASTRO CAN BE FOUND AT
amazon.com/author/sorceresscagliastro

www.cagliastrotheironring.com

CONTACT INFORMATION

For author information or for submission guidelines for North Sea Tales please visit

www.northseatales.com or contact

northseatales440@gmail.com

For your Sorcery Requirements, Readings/Consultations, to become a

student of the Science of Sorcery, or for information about THE FIRM...
sorceresscagliastro@gmail.com

BLANK PAGE FOR NOTES

BLANK PAGE FOR NOTES

The recording for ALL Sedations and other classes as well are soon to be available.

Visit www.cagliastrotheironring.com or contact sorceresscagliastro@gmail.com

Printed in Great Britain
by Amazon

37138848R00046